For my parents

Checklist compiled by Stuart Cooper

First U.S. edition

First published in Great Britain by Walker Books Ltd as
WHERE'S WALLY NOW?

Library of Congress Catalog Card No. 88-80340

ISBN 0–316–34292–0

20 19 18 17 16 15 14 13

Printed and bound by L.E.G.O., Vicenza, Italy

FIND WALDO NOW

MARTIN HANDFORD

Little, Brown and Company
Boston   Toronto   London

THE ABSOLUTELY HUGE AND ENORMOUSLY INTERESTING BOOK OF CAVEMEN, CAVE WOMEN, CAVE DOGS AND ALL SORTS OF EXTREMELY SAVAGE STONE-AGE BEASTS.

HI THERE, BOOK WORMS! WELL I'LL TELL YOU THIS FOR NOTHING – SOME BITS OF HISTORY ARE GREAT, FANTASTIC, JUST AMAZING! I SIT HERE READING ALL THESE BOOKS ABOUT THE WORLD LONG AGO, AND IT'S LIKE RIDING A TIME-MACHINE. WITH A LITTLE IMAGINATION I CAN REALLY GO PLACES. WOW! PHEW! IT'S WILD! WHY NOT TRY IT FOR YOURSELVES, WALDO FOLLOWERS? JUST FIND ME IN EACH PICTURE AND FOLLOW ME THROUGH TIME!

Waldo

4,578 YEARS AGO

THE RIDDLE OF THE PYRAMIDS

The Ancient Egyptians were very clever people who loved goats, cats and sphinx, and who invented pyramids. They built several huge pyramids in the desert. But now no one can remember why. Were they adventure playgrounds for Egyptian mummies and babies, or were they houses without doors or windows? To answer those questions and to find me can be as hard as a camel's hump.

2,000 YEARS AGO

FVN AND GAMES IN ANCIENT ROME

THE ROMANS SPENT MOST OF THEIR TIME FIGHTING, CONQVERING, LEARN-ING LATIN AND MAKING ROADS. THEY ALWAYS HAD GAMES AT THE COLISEVM. THEIR FAVORITE GAMES WERE FIGHTING, CHARIOT RACING, FIGHTING, AND FEEDING CHRISTIANS TO THE LIONS. WHEN THE CROWD GAVE A GLADIATOR THE THVMBS DOWN, IT MEANT KILL YOVR OPPO-NENT. THVMBS VP MEANT LET HIM GO. THVMBS VP FOR YOV IF YOV CAN FIND ME AT THE GAMES.

1,003 YEARS AGO

ON TOUR
WITH THE
VIKINGS

At høme, the Vikings were quiet peøple whø liked knitting, cheese tåsting and børing things like thåt. But øn tøur, they went wild. They put øn their best hørned håts and såiled åcross the seå, singing and shøuting like måd. If yøu heård them cøming, it wås best tø run awåy. But døn't yøu run awåy beføre yøu find me.

800 YEARS AGO

he End of the Crusades

After 200 years of fierce argument with the Saladins and Paladins, who would not tell them the way to Jerusalem, the Crusaders finally ran out of clean T-shirts, so they came home. For years afterward they dined out on stories of the castles they had battered and besieged and the fascinating people they had thrown rocks at. Go on your own crusade to find me.

600 YEARS AGO

ONCE UPON A SATURDAY MORNING

The Middle Ages were a very merry time to be alive, especially on Saturdays. Short skirts and striped tights were in fashion for men; everybody knew lots of jokes; there was widespread juggling, jousting, archery, jesting and fun. But if you got into trouble, the Middle Ages could be miserable. For the man in the stocks or the pillory or about to lose his head, Saturday morning was no laughing matter. Don't joke around, look for me here.

THE LAST DAYS OF THE AZTECS

The Aztecs lived in sunny Mexico and were rich and strong and liked swinging from poles pretending to be eagles. They also liked making human sacrifices to their gods, so it was best to agree with everything they said. The Spanish were also rich and strong and some of them, called conquistadores, came to Mexico to find gold. They thought the Aztecs a complete nuisance. Get swinging and find me in Mexico.

400 YEARS AGO

Is red better than blue? What do you mean your poem about cherry blossoms is better than mine? Shall we have another cup of tea? Over difficult questions such as these, the Japanese fought fiercely for hundreds of years. The fiercest fighters of all were the samurai, who wore flags on their backs so that their mommies could find them. The fighters without flags were called ashigaru. I don't have a flag either, but find me anyway.

250 YEARS AGO

BEING A PIRATE
(Shiver me timbers!)

It really was a lot of fun being a pirate, especially if you were very hairy and didn't have much in the way of brains. It also helped if you had only one leg, or one eye, or two noses, and had a pirate's hat with your name tag sewn inside and a treasure map and a rusty cutlass. Once there were lots of pirates, but they died out in the end because too many of them were men. Shiver me timbers and find me here.

100 YEARS AGO

THE GOLD RUSH

At the end of the nineteenth century large numbers of AMERICANS were frequently seen to be RUSHING toward HOLES in the ground, hoping to find GOLD. Most of them never even found the holes in the ground. But at least they all got EXERCISE and FRESH AIR, which kept them HEALTHY. And health is more important than GOLD . . . isn't it? You get the GOLD if you can spot me.

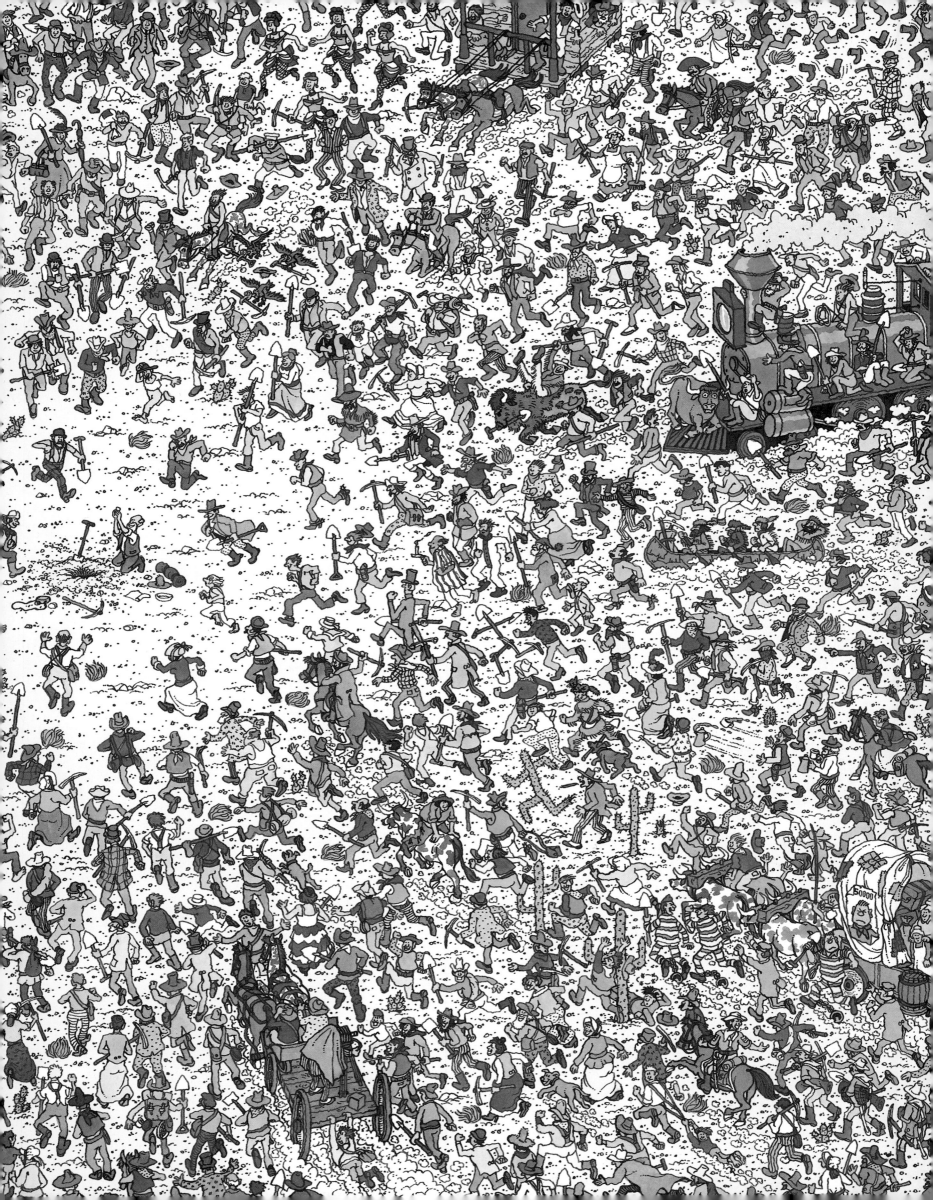

WALDO IS LOST
IN THE FUTURE!
FIND HIM! RESCUE HIM!
WALDO'S BOOKS ARE LOST
IN THE PAST! FIND THEM!
RESCUE THEM! THERE'S ONE
LOST IN EACH PICTURE.
GO BACK AND LOOK FOR THEM!
WHERE'S WALDO?
FIND WALDO NOW.

THE GREAT FIND WALDO NOW CHECKLIST
Hundreds more things for time travelers to look for!

THE STONE AGE

- Four cavemen swinging into trouble
- An accident with an axe
- A great invention
- A Stone-Age rodeo
- Boars chasing a man
- Men chasing a boar
- A romantic caveman
- A mammoth squirt
- A man who has overeaten
- A bear trap
- A mammoth in the river
- A fruit stall
- Charging woolly rhinos
- A big cover-up
- A trunk holding a trunk
- A knockout game of baseball
- A rocky picture show
- An upside-down boar
- A spoilt dog
- A lesson on dinosaurs
- A very scruffy family
- Some dangerous spear fishermen

THE RIDDLE OF THE PYRAMIDS

- An upside-down pyramid
- An upside-down sarcophagus
- A group of posing gods
- Two protruding hands
- Two protruding feet
- A fat man and his picture
- Seventeen protruding tongues
- Stones defying gravity
- Egyptian vandals
- Egyptian graffiti
- A man sweeping dirt under a pyramid
- A thirsty sphinx
- A runaway block of stone
- A loud blast
- A happy leopard
- A picture firing an arrow
- A careless water-carrier
- Sunbathers in peril
- A messy milking session
- A mummy and a baby
- Pyramids of sand

FUN AND GAMES IN ANCIENT ROME

- A charioteer who has lost his chariot
- Coliseum cleaners
- An unequal contest with spears
- A winner who is about to lose
- A lion with good table manners
- A deadly set of wheels
- Lion cubs being teased
- Four shields that match their owners
- A pyramid of lions
- Lions giving the paws down
- A leopard chasing a leopard skin
- A piggyback puncher
- An awful musician
- A painful fork-lift
- A horse holding the reins
- A leopard in love
- A Roman keeping count
- A gladiator losing his sandals

ON TOUR WITH THE VIKINGS

- A happy figurehead
- Figureheads in love
- A man being used as a club
- A tearful sheep
- Two hopeless hiding places
- Childish Vikings
- A beard with a foot on it
- An eagle posing as a helmet
- A sailor tearing a sail
- A heavily armed Viking
- A ride on a braid
- Three spears being beheaded
- A burning behind
- A bent boat
- A frightened figurehead
- Locked horns
- A helmet with spiders
- A helmet of smoke
- A bullfight

THE END OF THE CRUSADES

- A cat about to be catapulted
- A man about to be catapulted
- A human bridge
- A key that's out of reach
- A message for the milkman
- A cauldron of boiling oil
- A battering-ram
- Crusaders caught by their necks
- A load of washing
- Two catapult catastrophes
- A catapult aiming the wrong way
- Three snakes
- A crusader fast asleep
- Crusaders soaking up the sun
- Flattened crusaders
- Rockfaces
- A crusader who broke a ladder
- A ticklish situation

ONCE UPON A SATURDAY MORNING

- A dirty downpour
- Archers missing the target
- A jouster sitting back to front
- A dog stalking a cat stalking some birds
- A long line of pickpockets
- A jouster who needs lots of practice
- A man making a bear dance
- A bear making a man dance
- Hats that are tied together
- Fruit and vegetable thieves
- An unexpected puddle
- A juggling jester
- A very long drink
- A heavily burdened beast
- Drunken friars
- A man scything hats
- An angry fish
- A ticklish torture
- Minstrels making an awful noise